In recognition of your performance

Johns Hopkins University

Physics Fair

HISTORICAL ANIMALS

HISTORICAL ANIMALS

The Dogs, Cats,
Horses, Snakes,
Goats, Rats,
Dragons, Bears,
Elephants,
Rabbits, and
Other Creatures
That Changed
the World

BY JULIA MOBERG

ILLUSTRATED BY JEFF ALBRECHT STUDIOS

imagine!
Publishing

For Sam and Clementine—J.M.

An Imagine Book
Published by Charlesbridge
85 Main Street, Watertown, MA 02472
(617) 926-0329
www.charlesbridge.com

Library of Congress Cataloging-in-Publication Data

Moberg, Julia, author.
  Historical animals: the dogs, cats, horses, snakes, goats, rats, dragons, bears, elephants, rabbits, and other creatures that changed the world / by Julia Moberg; illustrated by Jeff Albrecht Studios.
       pages cm
"An Imagine Book."
Includes index.
ISBN 978-1-62354-048-7
1. Animals and history—Juvenile literature. 2. Animals and civilization—History—Juvenile literature. I. Jeff Albrecht Studios, illustrator. II. Title.
  QL85.M63 2015
  590.9—dc23
                                              2014018171

2 4 6 8 10 9 7 5 3 1

For information about custom editions, special sales, premium and corporate purchases, please contact Charlesbridge Publishing at specialsales@charlesbridge.com

Through history we learn
About many different things:
The pyramids, the moon landing,
And famous queens and kings.
Yet a certain population
Rarely gets its due:
Animals, you see,
Have left their paw prints, too!
The dog that saved Napoleon
And Mozart's starling bird
Both transformed the world,
But their stories go unheard.
Jane Goodall's chimpanzees,
Isaac Newton's cats,
A mongoose standing trial,
Some deadly fleas and rats,
A gorilla that can sign,
An elephant that wowed—
These tales and many more
All begin right now . . .

Table of Contents

Ramesses II

A lioness was captured
By Ramesses the Great,
Who decided to keep
The cat as a mate.
With claws that were sharp
And teeth that could maim,
Slayer of His Enemies
Was the cat's name.
To frighten his foes
He took her to war,
And people would scatter
When they heard her roar!

DID YOU KNOW?

* Ramesses's lioness was by his side during his famous battle at Kadesh against the Hittites.
* Cats were an important part of Egyptian society and religion. After they died, they were often mummified just like humans.
* The Egyptian goddess Mafdet had the head of a lion. People believed she protected them from poisonous animals, like snakes.
* On average, a male lion weighs about four hundred pounds. A female lion (or lioness) weighs around three hundred pounds.
* A male lion's roar can be heard up to five miles away.
* Hunting is usually done by lionesses in groups of two or three.

HISTORICAL STATS

FULL NAME: Ramesses II

NICKNAME: Ramesses the Great

BORN: 1303 BCE (Egypt)

DIED: July or August 1213 BCE (Egypt)

OCCUPATION: Third Egyptian pharaoh during the Nineteenth Dynasty

CLAIM TO FAME: Thought to be the greatest pharaoh of all time

TELL ME MORE!

* Ramesses II built many temples and structures throughout Egypt that still exist today.
* Many historians believe that Ramesses was the pharaoh from the Bible whom Moses freed the Israelites from.
* Ramesses II's principle wife (yes, he had several!) was Queen Nefertari. She participated in politics, foreign affairs, and went with her husband on important journeys.

Alexander the Great

At the age of thirteen,
Alexander the Great
Managed to tame
An untamable mate:
Bucephalus! A horse
Who stayed by his side,
And for thirty odd years
Into battle they'd ride.
But while fighting a war
One fateful spring day,
Bucephalus was hurt
And could no longer neigh.
Alex founded a city
To honor his pet,
The lifelong companion
He'd never forget.

DID YOU KNOW?

* Alexander's father, King Philip II, didn't want to keep Bucephalus because he was too wild. After Alexander was the only person able to tame the horse, Bucephalus was given to him as a gift.

* Bucephalus most likely died at the Battle of the Hydaspes in 326 BCE in what is now Pakistan.

* The city that Alexander founded in honor of his horse was called Bucephala (the modern-day town of Jalalpur Sharif, Pakistan).

* A statue of Alexander and Bucephalus was recently built in Skopje, the capital of Macedonia.

* Horses have been used in war for over five thousand years.

TELL ME MORE!

* Alexander the Great was one of the greatest military commanders in history.

* When he was a teenager, Alexander studied under the Greek philosopher Aristotle.

* After conquering Egypt, he founded the capital city Alexandria.

* Nobody is certain how Alexander the Great died, but many believe he was poisoned.

HISTORICAL STATS

FULL NAME: Alexander III of Macedon

NICKNAME: Alexander the Great

BORN: Around July 20, 356 BCE (Pella, Macedonia [now Greece])

DIED: June 10 or 11, 323 BCE (Babylon, Persia [now Iran])

OCCUPATIONS: King of Macedonia, Pharaoh of Egypt, King of Persia, and King of Asia

CLAIM TO FAME: *Never* lost a battle

Ptolemy II

A polar bear was
The king's favorite pet.
He led many parades,
Despite all the sweat.
But one has to wonder
How a polar bear came
To Egypt, a country
As hot as a flame!

DID YOU KNOW?

* The polar bear was kept at King Ptolemy's private zoo in Alexandria, Egypt.

* Typically, polar bears live in arctic climates. In ancient times, however, polar bears may not have been limited to those areas; they may have been able to survive wherever there was a substantial food supply.

* The Romans liked to watch polar bears chase seals around flooded arenas for entertainment.

* Polar bears' fur is transparent, not white, and the skin underneath is actually black. The fur appears white because of the way the sun reflects off of it.

* In 1973, the United States, Canada, Denmark, Norway, and the Soviet Union signed an agreement to protect polar bears from extinction.

* All polar bears are left-handed.

HISTORICAL STATS

FULL NAME: Ptolemy II Philadelphus

BORN: 309 BCE (Kos, Greece)

DIED: January 29, 246 BCE (Egypt)

OCCUPATION: King of Ptolemaic Egypt

CLAIM TO FAME: Prevented the Gauls from seizing Egypt

TELL ME MORE!

* A big supporter of the arts, Ptolemy II built the Great Library of Alexandria.

* He strengthened trade along the Mediterranean and boosted Egypt's economy by constructing new cities on the coast of the Red Sea.

* King Ptolemy II built many temples throughout Egypt.

* During his rule, Egypt was both wealthy and powerful.

Cleopatra

While being held captive,
Cleopatra knew
Her future was bleak
While Octavian ruled.
So she smuggled a cobra
In a basket of figs
And asked it to bite her,
And so the snake did.
The venom did kill her,
Just like she'd planned,
And Octavian no longer
Had the upper hand.

DID YOU KNOW?

* Cleopatra was taken prisoner by the Romans after losing the Battle of Actium. She knew that she would most likely be killed by the Roman ruler, Octavian, and she didn't want to give him the satisfaction.

* While Cleopatra's death is one of history's most well-known suicides, historians question whether she did, in fact, die at the hands of a cobra or if she poisoned herself.

* Cobras are able to lift their heads high off the ground. This helps them look for food.

* Cobras are carnivores. They eat birds, bird eggs, small mammals, and other snakes.

* A cobra's venom contains a strong neurotoxin that attacks its victims' nervous systems.

* The best way to treat a venomous snakebite is with antivenom.

HISTORICAL STATS

FULL NAME: Cleopatra VII Philopator

NICKNAME: Cleopatra

BORN: Late 69 BCE (Alexandria, Egypt)

DIED: August 12, 30 BCE (Alexandria, Egypt)

OCCUPATION: Pharaoh of Egypt

CLAIM TO FAME: The last pharaoh to rule Egypt

TELL ME MORE!

* Cleopatra was a member of the Ptolemaic dynasty, a family of Greek descent that ruled Egypt for three hundred years.

* Cleopatra and her brother, Ptolemy VIII, struggled for the Egyptian throne. In 48 BCE, the Roman dictator Julius Caesar helped Cleopatra defeat Ptolemy. They fell in love and had a child together.

* She fell in love with Mark Antony, one of three leaders who took over after Caesar was assassinated. Together they set out to defeat another Roman leader, Octavian.

* Octavian was victorious and took control of Egypt.

Virgil

When the government wanted
To seize all his land,
The Roman poet Virgil
Came up with a plan.
According to law
They could not touch
Land that contained
Dead bodies and such.
So he planned a big funeral
For one of his pets:
A housefly he claimed
He would never forget.

DID YOU KNOW?

* At the time, the government was confiscating land belonging to the rich and giving it to war veterans. The only exception was land that contained gravesites.
* Virgil's funeral for his pet fly worked, and in the end he was able to keep his land.
* For the event, Virgil hired an orchestra, invited celebrities, and had a poetry reading.
* Virgil spent about 800,000 sesterces on his fly's funeral.
* Houseflies get their name from being the most common flies found in homes.
* On average, houseflies live for twenty to thirty days.
* Houseflies can only eat liquids. They can turn solids into liquids by spitting or vomiting on them first.

HISTORICAL STATS

FULL NAME: Publius Vergilius Maro

NICKNAME: Virgil

BORN: October 15, 70 BCE (Cisalpine Gaul, Roman Republic [now Italy])

DIED: September 21, 19 BCE (Brundisium, Roman Empire [now Italy])

OCCUPATION: Poet

CLAIM TO FAME: Wrote the epic poem *The Aeneid*

TELL ME MORE!

* Virgil is considered to be the greatest Roman poet of all time.
* Virgil's epic poem, *The Aeneid*, tells the story of Aeneas, a Trojan who traveled to Italy and founded the city of Rome.
* *The Aeneid* took him eleven years to write.
* In the end, Virgil was not happy with *The Aeneid*. Before he died he left instructions for the manuscript to be destroyed, but his heirs published it anyway.
* *The Aeneid* is often compared to Homer's *The Iliad* and *The Odyssey*.
* Legend has it that after his death Virgil's bones protected the city of Naples. Attackers suffered from plagues of flies when they tried to enter the city.

Nero

At the grand Colosseum
While watching the fights,
The emperor Nero
Saw a great sight:
A tiger that snarled
And slashed with big claws.
Wreaking havoc on all,
She received great applause.
Nero watched as her fighting
Brought fear to the crowd.
She's mine. I must have her,
The emperor vowed.
So she went to live
Inside the palace gates,
And if you stepped out of line
You'd receive a grave fate.

DID YOU KNOW?

* Nero named the tigress Phoebe and had a golden cage built for her at the palace.
* Phoebe often ate dinner with the emperor at his table.
* Tigers are the largest wild cats in the world, sometimes weighing up to 720 pounds.
* Unlike other members of the cat family, tigers love water and will soak in streams to cool off.
* Tigers hunt at night.

TELL ME MORE!

* Nero improved the cultural life of the Roman Empire by building theaters and holding athletic games.
* During his reign, a great fire swept through Rome and destroyed much of the city. Historians wonder if Nero himself may have started the fire.
* Remembered as a brutal ruler, Nero used to persecute Christians by wrapping them in animal skins and throwing them to the lions.

HISTORICAL STATS

FULL NAME: Nero Claudius Caesar Augustus Germanicus

NICKNAME: Nero

BORN: December 15, 37 CE (Antium, Italy)

DIED: June 9, 68 CE (outside Rome, Italy)

OCCUPATION: Roman Emperor

CLAIM TO FAME: One of the most brutal emperors in classical Roman culture

Attila the Hun

During his reign,
Attila was vicious.
His desire for power
Was rather ambitious.
The Romans, the Gauls,
The Italians, too,
He'd go after anyone—
Perhaps even you!
Everyone feared him
Because by his side
An army of dogs
Into battle would ride.
These formidable dogs
Would snarl and maim,
Causing the enemy
To retreat back in shame.

HISTORICAL STATS

FULL NAME: Attila

NICKNAME: Attila the Hun

BORN: Unknown

DIED: 453 CE (present-day Hungary)

OCCUPATION: Ruler of the Hunnic Empire

CLAIM TO FAME: Conquered and attacked his way through Eastern and Central Europe

DID YOU KNOW?

- The dogs Attila the Hun used in battle were large Molossian dogs, precursors of mastiffs.
- Molossian dogs most likely originated from Tibet or northern India.
- Mastiffs are considered to be the largest breed in the world. A mastiff can weigh 220 pounds or more.
- In 1989, a mastiff named Zorba was named the world's heaviest dog by *The Guinness Book of World Records*, weighing 323 pounds.

TELL ME MORE!

- Originally descendants from a tribe of Mongolians, the Huns settled in the area known today as Hungary.
- Attila murdered his own brother in order to rule the Hun empire by himself.
- Attila the Hun may have died from a nosebleed on the night of his wedding. Some historians believe the nosebleed was caused by heavy drinking.
- Legend has it Attila's body was placed inside a gold coffin. The gold coffin was then placed inside a silver coffin. And after that, the silver coffin was placed inside a coffin made of iron.
- Supposedly the men who were sent to bury Attila were killed when they got back so that nobody would know the location of his burial place. To this day, his remains are one of the world's most important lost treasures.

Kaldi

Kaldi, a goat herder,
Was out with his goats.
On an African mountain,
They grazed and ate oats.
When suddenly they stumbled
Upon a tall tree
With shiny green leaves
And bright red berries.
The goats chomped away,
And when they were done
One of the goats
Took off on a run!
Some of them danced
And jumped all around.
Others did handstands
And flipped upside down.
Well, maybe not handstands . . .
But their energy spree
Was due to caffeine
From the coffee tree!

DID YOU KNOW?

* Kaldi took the berries to a monk at a nearby monastery, who made a drink with them. He noticed it kept him awake during evening prayer and shared it with the other monks. Soon, knowledge of the berries began to spread.

* The story of Kaldi and his goats is just that: a story. No concrete evidence exists that proves this is what occurred. But the myth has been passed down through the centuries.

* In bright lights, goats' pupils turn rectangular. Because of this, their vision spans 320–360 degrees, and they can see all around them.

* Bucks (male goats) have scent glands around the bases of their horns.

HISTORICAL STATS

FULL NAME: Kaldi

BORN: Sometime during the ninth century CE (Ethiopia)

DIED: Sometime during the ninth century CE (Ethiopia)

OCCUPATION: Goat herder

CLAIM TO FAME: With his herd of goats, discovered the coffee tree

TELL ME MORE!

* The coffee bean is actually a seed that is found inside a bright red berry on the coffee tree.

* Hawaii is the only state in the United States that grows coffee.

* Coffee is the second most traded commodity on our planet. Oil is the first.

Marco Polo

In the year twelve seventy-one CE,
Marco Polo took to the sea
And traveled to exotic lands
Through forests of trees and desert sands.
He wrote down everything he saw,
From wild beasts to rare macaws.
In China he saw quite a sight,
A sight that gave him quite a fright!
Huge serpents, thirty feet in length,
Three claws per arm with unseen strength,
Jaws wide enough to swallow man,
And teeth so large, they'd crush trash cans.
In caverns they would spend their days;
At night they'd leave to hunt their prey.
Big and strong and long and green,
Dragons were what he claimed he'd seen.

DID YOU KNOW?

* In his book, *The Travels of Marco Polo*, he recorded seeing "huge serpents." To this day, historians are baffled by his description. Did humans and dinosaur-like reptiles coexist? Or did he merely see a crocodile or Komodo dragon?

* Dragons of legend are similar to actual beasts that lived in the past.

* Dragons are an important part of many Chinese festivals, including Chinese New Year.

* Capable of reaching ten feet long and about three hundred pounds, the Komodo dragon is the largest lizard in the world.

* An adult Komodo dragon can eat up to 80 percent of its body weight in a single feeding.

TELL ME MORE!

* The Silk Road that Marco Polo traveled on is a four-thousand-mile route that links traders and merchants from China to the Mediterranean Sea. It gets its name from the Chinese silk trade, which began during the Han Dynasty (206 BCE–220 CE).

* The popular swimming pool game Marco Polo was named after the explorer. Legend has it he didn't know where he was going when he set out on his travels, just like the child who is "it" and has to remain blindfolded.

* Marco Polo inspired many explorers, including Christopher Columbus.

HISTORICAL STATS

FULL NAME: Marco Polo
BORN: 1254 CE (Venice, Italy)
DIED: January 8–9, 1324 CE (Venice, Italy)
OCCUPATIONS: Merchant, explorer
CLAIM TO FAME: Traveled the entire Silk Road, from Eastern Europe to Northern China

The Black Death

Back in the Middle Ages
When life was hard and grim,
A crisis came about
When a plague of death swept in.
From China into Russia
The plague spread very quickly;
Then through the rest of Europe
People started feeling sickly.
Some thought sewer rats
Were the ones to blame,
But turns out fleas were guilty
And deserved the shame!
Fleas lived upon rats' bodies,
Completely out of sight,
Then would pounce on humans
And deliver deadly bites.

HISTORICAL STATS

FULL NAME: Bubonic plague

NICKNAME: The Black Death

BORN: 1330s BCE (Mongolia)

OCCUPATION: Killer of millions

CLAIM TO FAME: Can kill a person in four days

DID YOU KNOW?

* The Black Death, or bubonic plague, is an infection of the lymphatic system. It's caused by the bite of an infected flea. The fleas are usually found on rats or mice, but they try to find other prey (such as people) when their rodent hosts die.

* A group of rats is called a mischief.

* Rats are surprisingly very clean animals. They spend hours each day grooming themselves and one another.

* Fleas can jump eight inches in the air, which is one hundred and fifty times their own height.

* Fleas can live up to one hundred days without eating.

TELL ME MORE!

* It is believed that the Black Death started in Mongolia in the early 1330s. It quickly spread into Russia and then throughout Europe.

* The Black Death killed an estimated 75 to 200 million people in the fourteenth century, including over a third of the European population.

* Doctors thought that the plague was caused by humid weather, decaying dead bodies, and poor sanitation. They recommended a good diet, rest, and relocating to noninfected areas for access to clean air. Sadly, this actually spread the infection to new areas.

* Today, bubonic plague is very rare. It is hardly found in the United States and is treatable with antibiotics.

Leonardo da Vinci

A painter, an architect,
The inventor of flight,
A sculptor, a scientist,
An astronomer at night.
He wore many different hats!
Yes, you get the gist.
But did you know Leo
Was an animal activist?
He would often go to markets
In Florence, Italy,
Buy caged birds,
And set them free.
This was a common occurrence;
It made him feel good
To help those who might
Be misunderstood.

HISTORICAL STATS

FULL NAME: Leonardo di ser Piero da Vinci

NICKNAME: Leonardo da Vinci

BORN: April 15, 1452 (Vinci, Italy)

DIED: May 2, 1519 (Amboise, France)

OCCUPATIONS: Italian Renaissance painter, sculptor, architect, musician, mathematician, engineer, inventor, anatomist, geologist, cartographer, botanist, writer

CLAIM TO FAME: One of many: Painted the *Mona Lisa*, arguably the most famous painting in the world

DID YOU KNOW?

* The caged birds Leonardo set free were typically meant to be bought for food or kept as pets.
* Leonardo questioned whether eating another living thing was right or wrong. He became a vegetarian later in life.
* A lover of animals, Leonardo used to study and sketch them, including dogs, cats, birds, horses, lions, bears, and even a dragon!
* Birds are the only animals that have feathers. They provide warmth and make flight possible.
* There are over 40 million pet birds in the United States.

TELL ME MORE!

* The "da Vinci" in Leonardo's name means "of Vinci," which is the town in Italy where he was born.
* Leonardo da Vinci was the first person to explain why the sky is blue. (It's because of the way air scatters light.)
* He was dyslexic and would sometimes write backward. During his life, he filled many notebooks with sketches and backward writing.
* It is believed that Leonardo was ambidextrous, meaning he was both left- and right-handed.
* Leonardo didn't have the chance to build many of his inventions, but several of the things he envisioned in the 1400s exist today, including parachutes and helicopters.
* Leonardo never married or had children.

Ferdinand Magellan

In the year fifteen twenty,
While exploring foreign lands,
Magellan spotted penguins
Standing on the sand.
Some would dive into the sea
While others sunned nearby.
The babies were quite small;
The grown-ups, two feet high.
Magellan was surprised
That creatures used to snow
Also liked the sun
And life as Latinos!

HISTORICAL STATS

FULL NAME: Ferdinand Magellan

BORN: 1480 (Sabrosa, Portugal)

DIED: April 27, 1521 (Mactan, Philippines)

OCCUPATION: Explorer

CLAIM TO FAME: His expedition, which was the first circumnavigation of the Earth

DID YOU KNOW?

* Magellan discovered the penguins on the coast of South America. They are known today as Magellanic penguins.

* Magellanic penguins live in Argentina, Chili, and the Falkland Islands.

* During the hot summer months, they shed the feathers around their eyes. In the colder months, the feathers grow back.

* Magellanic penguins eat fish, squid, and crustaceans.

TELL ME MORE!

Magellan was a Portuguese explorer. He served King Charles I of Spain, who sent him on a journey in search of the "Spice Islands" (the Maluku Islands in Indonesia).

* Magellan's great expedition from 1519–1522 set sail in the Atlantic Ocean. It was the first to circumnavigate the Earth.

* Magellan discovered a passageway from the Atlantic Ocean to the Pacific Ocean. Today it is called the Strait of Magellan.

* On the long journey around the globe, the sailors sometimes ate rats and sawdust to survive.

* Magellan didn't complete the expedition, but was killed in the Philippines during the Battle of Mactan. Around forty of his men also died during the battle.

* In the end, only eighteen sailors completed the full journey around the world. Their ship was captained by Juan Sebastián del Cano.

Isaac Newton

Isaac Newton owned cats,
According to lore,
Cats that would scratch
At his office door.
But while he was working
Isaac did find
This habit of theirs
Disrupted his mind.
So he cut two small holes,
And with the greatest of ease,
The cats could now come
And go as they pleased!
Many men question
While others insist
These pet doors were
The first to exist.

HISTORICAL STATS

Full Name: Sir Isaac Newton

Born: December 25, 1642 (Woolsthorpe, England)

Died: March 20, 1727 (London, England)

Occupations: Physicist, mathematician

Claim to Fame: Discovering the law of gravity

DID YOU KNOW?

* It is not known for certain if Isaac Newton invented the pet door. Some historians claim he didn't even own cats! However, to this day, two plugged holes are in the door of the office at the University of Cambridge where Newton once worked.

* Newton may have also had a dog named Diamond. Rumor has it the dog knocked over a candle and set fire to Newton's manuscripts and notes.

* There are more than 500 million domestic cats worldwide.

* Cats have powerful night vision.

TELL ME MORE!

* Newton's law of gravity describes the attraction between bodies with mass. According to legend, he got his inspiration when he saw an apple fall from a tree on his farm.

* Newton's three laws of motion explain how movement on Earth and in space works. For instance, why a resting object—such as a ball—will remain still until an outside force acts on it (someone kicks it).

* In an effort to study optics, Newton stuck a needle in his eye socket because he was curious as to what would happen. During the experiment, he saw several white, dark, and colored circles. His eye was not hurt in the process.

* To combat criminals counterfeiting Britain's currency, Newton was made warden at the Royal Mint. He took to the streets of London in disguise to root out counterfeiters. He also had all coins recalled, melted, and remade into a harder-to-counterfeit design. You know the rough edges on a quarter? Those were introduced by Newton on English coins.

Wolfgang Amadeus Mozart

While writing his Concerto
Number 17 in G,
Mozart went into a pet store
Whistling merrily.
When a starling whistled back,
Mimicking the tune,
Mozart bought him on the spot
And brought him home to croon.
There Mozart would compose
As the starling sang along.
For three whole years they worked
Together on the song.

HISTORICAL STATS

FULL NAME: Wolfgang Amadeus Mozart

BORN: January 27, 1756 (Salzburg, Austria)

DIED: December 5, 1791 (Vienna, Austria)

OCCUPATION: Classical composer

CLAIM TO FAME: One of the greatest
composers of all time

DID YOU KNOW?

* Mozart's bird was a European starling. When it passed away, Mozart held an elaborate funeral for his pet and wrote a commemorative poem in the bird's honor.

* European starlings are native to Europe, Asia, and North Africa. They were first introduced to North America in 1890, when one hundred starlings were released in New York City's Central Park.

* Today, European starlings are found on every continent except Antarctica.

* They eat seeds, insects, plants, and fruit.

TELL ME MORE!

* Mozart began piano lessons when he was four years old. By the age of five he was composing short works of music.

* At the age of six, Mozart began traveling and playing concerts throughout Europe.

* The Archduchess Maria Antonia, the future Marie Antoinette, attended a concert at Schönbrunn Palace in Vienna. After his performance, Mozart jumped into her lap and asked her to marry him.

* Mozart completed his first symphony at the age of eight. At thirteen, he composed his first opera.

* Some of Mozart's greatest works include *The Magic Flute* and *Don Giovanni*, operas that are still performed worldwide today.

Napoleon Bonaparte

Napoleon Bonaparte
Took to sea one night.
He sailed from Elba isle
Till France was in his sight.
But then he fell overboard
And almost broke a limb.
The future fate of France
Was looking rather grim!
Fortunately, a nearby dog
Jumped in and saved the day:
Grabbed Napoleon with his teeth
And pulled him from harm's way.
They floated till help came
Once darkness finally ceased.
Sadly we don't know the name
Of this heroic beast.

HISTORICAL STATS

FULL NAME: Napoleon Bonaparte

BORN: August 15, 1769 (Ajaccio, Corsica, France)

DIED: May 5, 1821 (Longwood, Saint Helena)

OCCUPATION: Emperor of France

CLAIM TO FAME: Conquered most of Europe

DID YOU KNOW?

✳ The dog that saved Napoleon belonged to a local fisherman. Some historians believe it may have been a Newfoundland.

✳ As emperor, Napoleon passed a law making it illegal for anyone to name their dog "Napoleon."

✳ In September 1816, Napoleon wrote: "If you do not like dogs, you do not like fidelity; you do not like those who are attached to you; and, therefore, you are not faithful."

✳ Napoleon's first wife, Josephine, had an orangutan that would join them at the table for meals.

✳ Newfoundland dogs originated in Newfoundland, Canada, and were used by fishermen to pull in their nets.

✳ One of the most famous Newfoundlands is Nana, the fictional nanny in *Peter Pan* by J. M. Barrie.

TELL ME MORE!

✳ In his portraits Napoleon is always in the same position: turned to the side with his hand inside his jacket.

✳ Napoleon has a reputation for being short, but in fact he was average height.

✳ Napoleon was also an author. He wrote a romance novel, *Clisson et Eugénie.*

✳ His wife Josephine changed her name from Rose because Napoleon didn't like it.

✳ Napoleon jailed thirteen Roman Catholic cardinals for not attending his second marriage.

Barry der Menschenretter

Barry der Menschenretter
Worked in the Alps
As a rescue dog
for those needing help.
From children to soldiers
To those who'd been injured,
Barry would find them
Even in a bad blizzard.
In the course of his life
He saved forty lives,
And even today
His legacy survives.
At the St. Bernard Hospice
Where Barry had been,
Today you will find
Some of his kin.

DID YOU KNOW?

* From 1800–1812, Barry lived at the St. Bernard Hospice, a monastery in the Pennine Alps in Switzerland.

* The dogs would find buried travelers, dig through the snow, and lie on top of the injured to provide warmth. Over the span of two hundred years, two thousand people were rescued by the dogs.

* Barry's body is preserved and exhibited in the Natural History Museum in Bern, Switzerland. There is a monument of him in the Cimetière des Chiens in Paris, France.

* St. Bernards are known for being smart, even-tempered, nonterritorial, obedient, loyal, and great with kids and other animals.

HISTORICAL STATS

FULL NAME: Barry der Menschenretter

BORN: 1800 (Great St. Bernard Hospice, Pennine Alps)

DIED: 1814 (Bern, Switzerland)

OCCUPATION: Mountain rescue dog for the Great St. Bernard Hospice

CLAIM TO FAME: Saved more than forty people during his lifetime

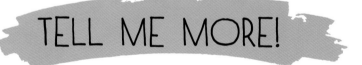

TELL ME MORE!

* The Great St. Bernard Pass in the Pennine Alps is the third-highest road pass in Switzerland.

* Since the early eighteenth century, monks living in the dangerous pass rescued travelers after bad snowstorms.

* A famous portrait by Jacques-Louis David in 1801 depicts Napoleon Bonaparte crossing the Great St. Bernard Pass.

* The Alps cover 65 percent of Switzerland's surface area. Switzerland is home to some of the most famous Alpine locations—the Matterhorn, the Eiger, and other high peaks and large glaciers.

Lewis and Clark

Lewis and Clark
Set out on a mission
To travel the country
On the president's commission.
They brought their dog, Seaman,
Along for the ride.
He was the first dog in history
To travel nationwide.
From sea to shining sea,
He braved the long trek.
He survived a beaver bite
And an Indian attack!
He chased and caught squirrels
That the men ate for food
And at night he watched out
For those who'd intrude.
Yes, Seaman was vital
To Lewis and Clark,
Which is why there are statues
Of him in state parks.

DID YOU KNOW?

* Meriwether Lewis purchased Seaman, a black Newfoundland, for twenty dollars in Pittsburgh, Pennsylvania.

* During the journey, Seaman suffered a beaver bite that injured an artery in his leg. Lewis and Clark stopped the bleeding and performed minor surgery on their pet's leg.

* During the trip back, Seaman was stolen by Native Americans. Lewis threatened to send armed men to kill them if they didn't return the dog. In the end, Lewis and Clark got the dog back without having to fight the tribe.

* Various monuments and statues of Seaman can be found throughout the United States.

* When traveling with a dog, make sure that they are wearing a collar with an ID tag that has your home address, a neighbor's telephone number, your mobile number, and/or the telephone number at your destination.

HISTORICAL STATS

FULL NAMES: Meriwether Lewis and William Clark

BORN: Lewis—August 18, 1774 (Ivy, Virginia); Clark—August 1, 1770 (Ladysmith, Virginia)

DIED: Lewis—October 11, 1809 (Hohenwald, Tennessee); Clark—September 1, 1838 (St. Louis, Missouri)

OCCUPATION: American explorers

CLAIM TO FAME: Led the first expedition to cross the western portion of the United States all the way to the Pacific coast

TELL ME MORE!

* The Lewis and Clark expedition was commissioned by President Thomas Jefferson shortly after the Louisiana Purchase in 1803. The goal of the expedition was to explore and map the new territory. The journey lasted from May 1804 to September 1806.

* Sacagawea, a Native American Indian, joined the expedition as an interpreter. She helped them peacefully trade with different tribes and also showed them which plants were edible.

Charles Darwin

Aboard the *HMS Beagle*
Darwin sailed around,
Then landed in the Galápagos
And was shocked by what he found.
Turns out that each island
Contained the same fauna:
Mockingbirds and tortoises,
Finches and iguanas.
When he looked much closer
He noticed their physiques:
Tortoises' diverse shells,
Finches' distinct beaks.
He set out to discover
How these divergences accrued.
Perhaps varied climates?
Or different types of food?
So Darwin crafted a theory
After much more inspection
About the origin of species
By means of natural selection.

HISTORICAL STATS

FULL NAME: Charles Robert Darwin

BORN: February 12, 1809 (Shrewsbury, Shropshire, England)

DIED: April 19, 1882 (Downe, Kent, England)

OCCUPATIONS: Naturalist, geologist

CLAIM TO FAME: Made huge discoveries in evolutionary theory

DID YOU KNOW?

* After studying the animals in the Galápagos Islands, Charles Darwin discovered that all species evolve from common ancestors. He published his theory in his book *On the Origins of Species by Means of Natural Selection.*

* While he was in college, Darwin joined the Gourmet Club, which would meet to eat uncommon animals such as hawk and owl. He continued this tradition during his travels, and while in the Galápagos Islands, he ate iguanas and tortoises.

* There are around fifteen types of finches in the Galápagos Islands. They are known today as Darwin's finches.

* Tortoises have the same life span as humans. Some can live from ninety to one hundred and fifty years old.

* Tortoises don't have teeth. Instead they have horned beaks, like birds.

TELL ME MORE!

* Darwin began to study medicine at the University of Edinburgh. He couldn't stand the sight of blood, though, so decided to study divinity instead.

* The Church of England verbally attacked Darwin after his theory of evolution was first published. One hundred and twenty-six years after his death, they officially apologized.

* Charles Darwin married his first cousin Emma, and together they had ten children.

* Every night, Darwin would play two games of backgammon with Emma. He kept score of every game they played.

Florence Nightingale

In Athens, Greece,
While out for a stroll,
Florence saw something
That clutched at her soul:
A small baby owl
Preparing to fly
Had fallen to earth
And almost did die.
Furthermore, some boys
Were tormenting the owl,
So Florence intervened
And shooed them with a scowl.
She picked up the bird,
Then nursed it to health,
And in doing so
Transformed herself.
She discovered her calling
From doing this deed
And went into nursing
To help those in need.

HISTORICAL STATS

Full Name: Florence Nightingale

Nickname: Lady with the Lamp

Born: May 12, 1820 (Florence, Italy)

Died: August 13, 1910 (London, England)

Occupation: Nurse

Claim to Fame: Changed the way hospitals were run with her work in nursing

DID YOU KNOW?

* Florence named her owl Athena. She used to carry her around in her pocket.

* There are around two hundred different owl species.

* Owls can turn their heads as far as 270 degrees.

* Owls are nocturnal animals, which means they are only active at night.

* A group of owls is called a parliament.

* Owls don't have teeth. They swallow small prey whole and tear larger prey into bite-size pieces.

TELL ME MORE!

* Florence Nightingale was the founder of modern nursing.

* Florence's parents were shocked when she told them she wanted to learn about nursing. At the time nurses came from poor families, and Florence's family was wealthy.

* During the Crimean War, she made a lot of changes to the hospital where she worked. She cleaned drains, improved drinking water, cleaned bandages before use, and set up a nursing timetable.

* The wounded soldiers called her the Lady with the Lamp because she used to walk the hospital wards at night to check on her patients.

* In 1959, Florence wrote a book about caring for the sick called *Notes on Nursing*.

* In 1860, she set up the Nightingale Training School for Nurses at St. Thomas' Hospital in London.

Alexander Graham Bell

Alexander Graham Bell
Had several careers:
Inventor, scientist,
Even engineer.
While studying sound
He tried a technique
On his own dog Trouve
And taught him to speak.
This led to the thing
For which he's most known,
His greatest invention . . .
The first telephone!

DID YOU KNOW?

* Alexander taught Trouve, a Skye Terrier, how to "talk" by manually manipulating the dog's lips and vocal cords to produce a variety of sounds.

* One sentence in particular that Trouve could "say" was "How are you, Grandmama?"

* Skye Terriers are one of the oldest kinds of terriers known today.

* During the nineteenth century, Queen Victoria of England owned several Skye Terriers and made the breed quite popular, especially among nobility.

TELL ME MORE!

* There is speculation as to whether Alexander Graham Bell did in fact invent the first telephone, or if he merely patented the first one. Some believe an Italian named Antonio Meucci invented the first "telettrofono" in 1854.

* Disinterested by school, Alexander dropped out when he was fifteen. Later in life he earned a series of honorary degrees from several colleges, including Harvard, Dartmouth, the University of Edinburgh, and more.

* Both his mother and wife were deaf. This peaked his interest in sound and speech.

* Alexander Graham Bell was good friends with Helen Keller. A deafblind person, Keller was an author, lecturer, and political activist.

* He helped found both the National Geographic Society and *National Geographic Magazine*.

* The first intelligible words spoken over his telephone were "Mr. Watson, come here. I want to see you."

HISTORICAL STATS

FULL NAME: Alexander Graham Bell

BORN: March 3, 1847 (Edinburgh, Scotland)

DIED: August 2, 1922 (Nova Scotia, Canada)

OCCUPATIONS: Scientist, inventor, engineer, innovator

CLAIM TO FAME: Possibly invented the first telephone

Theodore Roosevelt

One day while hunting,
Teddy Roosevelt refused
To shoot a small bear cub
And made the day's news.
When a toy company saw
No blood had been shed,
They had an idea
And grabbed needle and thread.
They found some fabric
That was brown and furry.
With stuffing and buttons,
They sewed in a hurry.
They put the stuffed toy
In the window with care
With a small little sign
That read TEDDY'S BEAR.

DID YOU KNOW?

* This infamous hunting trip took place in 1902 in Mississippi. Roosevelt had been invited on the expedition by Mississippi governor Andrew H. Longino.

* The Brooklyn shopkeeper Morris Michtom sold the first "Teddy's bear" in 1902.

* The Steiff Company in Germany also produced a stuffed bear that they exhibited in 1903 at the Leipzig Toy Fair. To this day, they claim they invented the teddy bear.

* Bear cubs stay with their mothers for the first two years of their lives. During this time they learn how to hunt for food and survive on their own.

HISTORICAL STATS

FULL NAME: Theodore Roosevelt, Jr.

NICKNAME: Teddy

BORN: October 27, 1858 (New York, New York)

DIED: January 6, 1919 (Oyster Bay, New York)

OCCUPATIONS: Author, explorer, historian, 26th president of the United States

CLAIM TO FAME: Ranked by scholars as one of the greatest US presidents

TELL ME MORE!

* Roosevelt is the only president to receive a Congressional Medal of Honor (for his heroic actions during the Spanish-American War). He also won the Nobel Prize for his work ending the Russo-Japanese War.

* He doubled the number of national parks in the country.

* After his presidency, Roosevelt embarked on an eleven-month hunting safari in Africa that was commissioned by the Smithsonian Institution. The animals Roosevelt trapped or shot became the foundation for the Smithsonian's National Museum of Natural History's collection.

A man named P. T. Barnum
Wanted to create
"The Greatest Show on Earth"
And take it state to state.
So for the show he purchased
Quite a heavy load:
An elephant from London,
The "largest in the world!"
But it wasn't easy
Feeding such a beast;
Every day they'd bring him
Quite a hefty feast.
First Jumbo would eat
Two hundred pounds of hay,
Fifteen loaves of bread,
And whiskey (which he'd spray).
Then a barrel of potatoes,
Some onions with the peels,
And two bushels of cereal.
It was quite a heavy meal!

DID YOU KNOW?

* In 1880, P. T. Barnum purchased Jumbo from the Royal Zoological Society for ten thousand dollars ($242,000 today).

* In his first ten days with the circus, Jumbo brought in thirty thousand dollars. During the first year, he made $1.5 million.

* Because of Jumbo's size, the word *jumbo* now means *large* or *big*.

* Jumbo tragically died on September 15, 1885, after being hit by a train locomotive. After his death, the elephant's skeleton continued to travel with the Barnum & Bailey Circus. His hide was stuffed and donated to Tufts University in Medford, Massachusetts.

* Jumbo is the official mascot of Tufts University.

* Despite popular myth, elephants do not eat peanuts. Peanuts are too high in fat and too small to be fed to captive elephants.

* Elephants have a sixth toe that is hidden beneath the foot.

HISTORICAL STATS

FULL NAME: Phineas Taylor Barnum

NICKNAME: P.T.

BORN: July 5, 1810 (Bethel, Connecticut)

DIED: April 7, 1891 (Bridgeport, Connecticut)

OCCUPATION: American showman and circus promoter

CLAIM TO FAME: Founded the Barnum & Bailey Circus

TELL ME MORE!

* P. T. Barnum's circus was created in Wisconsin and was originally named P. T. Barnum's Grand Traveling Museum, Menagerie, Caravan, and Hippodrome.

* James Anthony Bailey owned the Cooper and Bailey Circus with a man named James E. Cooper.

* Barnum and Bailey combined their shows, and the Barnum & Bailey Circus opened their tent in 1882.

* After Barnum and Bailey passed away, the circus was purchased by the Ringling Brothers and became known as the Ringling Bros. and Barnum & Bailey Circus.

Punxsutawney Phil

In the state of Pennsylvania
A groundhog soundly sleeps.
He hibernates all winter
And barely makes a peep.
He yawns when he wakes up,
He stretches, his muscles flex,
And the town of Punxsutawney
Awaits what happens next.
He heads outside to see
If winter's come and gone.
He feels the frigid cold
And gives another yawn.
But suddenly he senses
The warmth of the sunlight.
He opens up his eyes to find
It really is quite bright.
He saunters through the snow
And dreams of May and June.
He can smell it in the air:
Spring will be here soon!

HISTORICAL STATS

FULL NAME: Punxsutawney Phil

BORN: Unknown

OCCUPATION: Weatherman

CLAIM TO FAME: Every February second, predicts whether there will be an early spring or six more weeks of winter

DID YOU KNOW?

* Every Groundhog Day, Punxsutawney Phil emerges from his home on Gobbler's Knob (a rural area just east of Punxsutawney, Pennsylvania). If Phil sees his shadow and returns to his hole, he predicts there will be six more weeks of winter. If he doesn't see his shadow, he predicts that spring will arrive early.

* According to the Punxsutawney Groundhog Club, Phil speaks his prediction to the club president in "Groundhogese," and then his prediction is translated for the world.

* The Groundhog Club claims that there has only been one Phil since the tradition started in 1887. Rumor has it he drinks "groundhog punch," which gives him seven more years of life.

* Groundhogs hibernate every year. Hibernation is a deep coma where the body temperature drops to a few degrees above freezing, the heart beats rapidly, blood scarcely flows, and breathing nearly stops.

TELL ME MORE!

* It is believed that Germans brought the tradition of Groundhog Day over when they settled in Pennsylvania in the early 1800s. They replaced the European hedgehog with a groundhog.

* Punxsutawney Phil and the town were portrayed in the 1993 comedy *Groundhog Day*, starring Bill Murray and directed by the late Harold Ramis.

* The Groundhog Club's Inner Circle is a group of gentlemen who are responsible for planning Groundhog Day. They wear matching black tuxedos and black top hats. They also feed and take care of Punxsutawney Phil.

Beatrix Potter

When she was just a child,
Beatrix never played
With other little children;
She stayed quite far away.
Her only true companions
Had furry hides and tails:
A hedgehog, a dormouse,
A spaniel, even snails!
Her favorite by far was
Her rabbit Peter Piper,
Who inspired her to draw
And become a famous writer.

HISTORICAL STATS

FULL NAME: Helen Beatrix Potter

BORN: July 28, 1866 (London, England)

DIED: December 22, 1943 (Near Sawry, England)

OCCUPATION: Children's book writer and illustrator

CLAIM TO FAME: Writing and illustrating *The Tale of Peter Rabbit*, which some regard as the first children's picture book

DID YOU KNOW?

* Beatrix Potter dreamt up the story of Peter Rabbit while writing letters to her late governess's ill son, Noel. They were based on one of her real-life rabbits, Peter Piper.

* Beatrix Potter's other rabbit, Benjamin Bouncer, inspired the character Benjamin Bunny.

* A female rabbit is called a doe, a male rabbit is called a buck, and a baby rabbit is called a kit or kitten.

* Rabbits have nearly 360-degree vision. They can see behind them without turning around.

TELL ME MORE!

* Beatrix Potter grew up in England. Because her parents feared she would catch germs from other children, she only played with her brother and the animals that lived around the family's cottage.

* She taught herself to draw and spent hours sketching and drawing her pets.

* Unable to find a publisher for *The Tale of Peter Rabbit*, Beatrix Potter originally published it herself in 1901.

* She published twenty-three books, all in a small format, suitable for children's hands.

Pelorus Jack

A dolphin named Jack
Helped many ships at sea
Down in New Zealand
In the nineteenth century.
In treacherous waters
He'd often lead the way
Through rocks and strong winds
Almost every day.
For twenty years he worked
And quickly rose to fame.
All around the world
He received much acclaim.
Newspapers would write
About Jack's many feats,
And a candy maker made
Chocolate Jack fish treats.
Tourists would travel
And give a big hurrah!
Hunters couldn't touch him;
He was protected by the law.
Still today the one thing
That remains a mystery
Is if he was a he at all—
He may have been a she!

DID YOU KNOW?

* Pelorus Jack, a Risso's dolphin, first appeared in 1888 when a ship approached the French Pass, a dangerous channel in New Zealand with rocks and strong currents. To the captain's amazement, the dolphin began to guide them through the narrow channel.

* He was named after Pelorus Sound, a body of water at the north of the South Island in New Zealand. Despite his name, Jack never actually lived in Pelorus Sound.

* Although he was called Jack, his sex was never determined.

* In 1904, someone aboard the *SS Penguin* tried to shoot Pelorus Jack with a rifle. Soon after, a law was passed to protect the dolphin. It is believed that he was the first sea creature ever to be protected by law.

* After his protection, worldwide publicity made the dolphin famous. Many tourists traveled to see him, as did the famous writers Mark Twain and Rudyard Kipling.

* Dolphins are very intelligent animals that communicate with one another by clicking, whistling, and making other sounds.

HISTORICAL STATS

FULL NAME: Pelorus Jack

BORN: Unknown

DIED: April 1912 (unknown)

OCCUPATION: Ships' guide

CLAIM TO FAME: Escorted ships through a dangerous channel of water

TELL ME MORE!

* Ships and boats are one of the oldest forms of transportation. The first boats were actually rafts, made from logs tied together.

* The difference between a boat and a ship is that boats are designed for rivers and other waterways while ships are built for seas and oceans.

Cher Ami

Cher Ami, which means
"Dear Friend" in French,
Was a carrier pigeon
Who served in the trench.
One day his unit
Received friendly fire
And needed some help
Or they would expire.
So they sent Cher Ami
To deliver a note.
For heaven's sake, stop it,
The US major wrote.
Through bullets he flew
Over twenty-five miles
And delivered the note!
His trip proved worthwhile.
One hundred and ninety-four
Men had been saved,
And afterward, Cher Ami
Met with much praise.

HISTORICAL STATS

FULL NAME: Cher Ami

BORN: Unknown

DIED: June 13, 1919 (Fort Monmouth, New Jersey)

OCCUPATION: Carrier pigeon

CLAIM TO FAME: Saved an entire battalion of men during World War I

DID YOU KNOW?

* On October 3, 1918, five hundred US soldiers were trapped on a hill behind enemy lines. They were being shot at by Allied forces.

* Carrier pigeons were sent for help. The first two pigeons were shot down, and only one, Cher Ami, remained.

* Cher Ami was dispatched with a note in a canister that read, *We are along the road parallel to 276.4. Our own artillery is dropping a barrage directly on us. For heaven's sake, stop it.*

* Cher Ami hurt his leg during the flight, and army medics worked long and hard to save his life. When he was better, he was put on a boat to the United States.

* He became the mascot for the Department of Service, and was awarded the Croix de Guerre Medal.

* On average, a carrier pigeon can fly fifty miles an hour.

TELL ME MORE!

* World War I began on June 28, 1914, when a Serbian terrorist shot Archduke Franz Ferdinand (heir to the Austro-Hungarian Empire). Austria-Hungary immediately declared war on Serbia.

* More than 65 million men from thirty countries fought in World War I and made up two opposing alliances: the Allies and the Central Powers.

* The Allies consisted of many countries, including Serbia, Russia, France, the British Empire, and the United States.

* The Central Powers included Germany, Austria-Hungary, Bulgaria, and the Ottoman Empire (modern-day Turkey).

* The Allies won the war, which officially ended on November 11, 1918.

Rin Tin Tin

At the end of World War I,
A soldier found a slew
Of hungry little puppies
And decided to keep two.
He named the girl Nanette,
And the boy was Rin Tin Tin.
Little did the soldier know
The legacy he'd bring.
After returning to the states,
It soon became quite clear
That Rin Tin Tin was destined
For the Hollywood frontier.
The dog went on to star
In movies galore,
Then radio and TV—
The people wanted more!
Every week he'd receive
Fan mail by the bunch.
He even had a chef
Who cooked him beef for lunch.
This rags-to-riches canine
Remains well known today,
And for other doggy actors,
He really paved the way.

HISTORICAL STATS

FULL NAME: Rin Tin Tin

BORN: September 1918 (Lorraine, France)

DIED: August 10, 1932 (Los Angeles, California)

OCCUPATION: Actor

CLAIM TO FAME: One of the first and greatest canine actors of all time.

DID YOU KNOW?

* The soldier, Lee Duncan, found a litter of German shepherds at an abandoned kennel in the Lorraine region of France. He kept two of them for himself, naming them Rin Tin Tin and Nanette after finger puppets that French children gave American soldiers.

* Rin Tin Tin's first role was in the 1923 film *Where the North Begins.* Afterward, he starred in several Warner Bros. films. In 1930, he landed his own radio show called *The Wonder Dog.*

* In 1932, Rin Tin Tin was replaced by his son, Rin Tin Tin, Jr., who went on to star in many films throughout the 1930s. When one dog could no longer perform, his descendant stepped in to fill his "paws."

* The current Rin Tin Tin is Rin Tin Tin XII, who travels the country and raises awareness for responsible pet ownership.

* The German shepherd breed originated in Germany, where they were first used to herd and protect flocks of sheep.

TELL ME MORE!

* When filming, neutral-colored dogs are preferred over white or black dogs because they don't require special lighting.

* Dog actors must recognize and respond to hand signals.

* Proper representation by an animal talent agency is recommended if you want your dog or pet to be an actor. Put together a portfolio that includes photographs and a list of the animal's skills and abilities. Be sure to list all the tricks he can perform!

Balto

In the town of Nome, Alaska,
Everyone was sick.
They needed some medicine
And needed it quick.
So a team of husky sled dogs
Was given the task
To deliver the treatment
And get it there fast.
A husky named Balto
Led his sled dog pack
Through a deadly blizzard
and kept them all on track.
Through the night they ran,
Racing at full speed
To make it there in time,
With Balto at the lead!

DID YOU KNOW?

✳ In 1925, a deadly diphtheria outbreak swept through the town of Nome, Alaska. The closest serum was in Seattle, Washington. The only aircraft available to deliver the medicine wasn't working, so it was decided to deliver the medicine via dog sled teams.

✳ On February 2, 1925, Norwegian Gunnar Kaasen drove his team, led by Balto, to Nome with the medicine.

✳ Afterward, Balto received lots of publicity for his efforts. Even President Calvin Coolidge personally thanked Balto.

✳ A statue of Balto was erected in New York's Central Park on December 17, 1925.

✳ Sled dogs can run at an average of twenty miles an hour.

✳ Breeds used as sled dogs include the Alaskan husky, the Alaskan malamute, the Siberian husky, the Canadian Eskimo Dog, the Chinook, the Greenland Dog, and others.

HISTORICAL STATS

FULL NAME: Balto

BORN: 1919 (Nome, Alaska)

DIED: March 14, 1933 (Cleveland, Ohio)

OCCUPATION: Sled dog

CLAIM TO FAME: Delivered a diphtheria antitoxin to combat an outbreak in Nome, Alaska

TELL ME MORE!

✳ Diphtheria is a bacterial infection that affects the throat and nose.

✳ In Colonial times, diphtheria plagued American settlers and wiped out half of the population. The disease also spread to Native American communities, sometimes affecting entire villages.

✳ Today diphtheria is a very rare disease. Most children are vaccinated at an early age to protect them from it.

✳ Washing your hands is the best way to prevent germs from spreading and to keep from getting sick.

Unsinkable Sam

A cat named Oskar
Who was black and white
Lived on a German ship
Attacked by Brits at night.
The ship went down,
But Oskar survived.
He was saved by the Brits,
And so he switched sides.
They called him Oscar,
With a *C*, not a *K*,
And many different sailors
Took care of the stray.
Then their boat sank, too,
And many men died.
But Oscar managed
To get out alive.
He then went to live
On another big boat,
But sadly it, too,
Did not stay afloat.
While it was sinking
Oscar did scram,
And soon become known
As Unsinkable Sam.

HISTORICAL STATS

FULL NAME: Oskar or Oscar

NICKNAME: Unsinkable Sam

BORN: Before 1941 (Germany)

DIED: 1955 (Belfast, Northern Ireland)

OCCUPATION: Ship's cat

CLAIM TO FAME: Survived three shipwrecks during World War II

DID YOU KNOW?

* The first ship Unsinkable Sam lived on was the German battleship the *Bismarck*. The second was the British destroyer the *HMS Cossack*. The third ship he called home was the British aircraft carrier the *HMS Ark Royal*.

* Coincidentally, the *HMS Ark Royal* was the ship that attacked the *Bismarck*, the cat's first home.

* Unsinkable Sam was transferred back to the United Kingdom and spent the rest of his life on land in Belfast, Ireland.

* Some historians question whether one cat could have survived all three shipwrecks.

* A group of cats is called a clowder or a glaring.

* A male cat is called a tom or gib, a female cat is called a queen or molly, and baby cats are called kittens.

TELL ME MORE!

* Sailors have a long tradition of keeping cats as pets. Not only do they provide companionship, they rid ships of rats and mice. These vermin are harmful because they eat the ship's food rations, gnaw through ropes, and spread disease.

* Some superstitious sailors believe that cats protect them by bringing good luck.

* It is believed that the ancient Egyptians were the first seafarers to keep cats as shipmates.

* Phoenician cargo ships were thought to have brought the first domesticated cat to Europe around 900 BCE.

Huberta

Huberta the hippo
Was basking quietly
In her watering hole
At her estuary
When suddenly she decided
To go for a walk
Through sandy beaches
Amongst river rocks.
Across South Africa
She walked for three years!
And crowds of people
Came out to cheer.
She soon became known
As the national pet
And made the headlines
In several gazettes.

HISTORICAL STATS

FULL NAME: Huberta

BORN: Unknown

DIED: April 1931 (East London, South Africa)

OCCUPATION: Adventurer

CLAIM TO FAME: Most famous animal in South Africa's history

DID YOU KNOW?

* In November 1928, Huberta left her home at the St. Lucia Estuary in the Zululand province of South Africa. She set off on a thousand-mile journey to the eastern edge of South Africa.

* Even though she was classified as "royal game" by the Natal Provincial Council and thus protected by law, she was shot by a group of hunters who were unaware of her fame. They were arrested and fined twenty-five pounds each.

* After her death, Huberta's body was sent to a taxidermist in London. When it returned to South Africa in 1932, it was greeted by more than twenty thousand fans. It can now be seen in the Amathole Museum in King William's Town.

* The word *hippopotamus* comes from Greek and means "river horse."

TELL ME MORE!

* South Africa is home to 10 percent of the world's known birds, fish, and plants and 6 percent of the world's mammals and reptiles.

* In 1910, the British created the country of South Africa by uniting four colonies. They passed laws that separated white people from black South Africans. This segregation was called apartheid and led to decades of conflict.

* In 1963, Nelson Mandela, head of the anti-apartheid African National Congress, was sentenced to life in prison. He was set free in 1990, and in 1994 became president of South Africa.

Sergeant Reckless

In nineteen fifty-two
During the Korean War,
A Mongolian mare named Reckless
Joined the Marine Corps.
Her job wasn't easy
During fighting time:
She delivered rounds of ammo
To soldiers on front lines.
Even when some shrapnel
Hit her in the eye,
Reckless kept on going
Till victory was nigh.

HISTORICAL STATS

FULL NAME: Ah Chim Hai (Korean for "Flame in the Morning")

NICKNAME: Sergeant Reckless

BORN: 1948 (Korea)

DIED: May 13, 1968 (Camp Pendleton, California)

OCCUPATION: Member of the United States Marine Corps

CLAIM TO FAME: One of America's greatest animal war heroes

DID YOU KNOW?

* During the Battle of Panmunjom-Vegas in 1953, Reckless traveled thirty-five miles and made fifty-one trips to resupply the front line units. She was wounded twice, but kept going.

* Reckless was promoted twice, first from corporal to sergeant and then again from sergeant to staff sergeant.

* Reckless would eat anything. Her favorite foods were scrambled eggs, pancakes, cake, candy, Coca-Cola, and poker chips!

* Her honors include two Purple Hearts, a Good Conduct Medal, a National Defense Service Medal, a Korean Service Medal, and a United Nations Service Medal, among others.

* She was named as one of America's one hundred all-time heroes by *Life* magazine.

* Horses sleep both lying down and standing up.

TELL ME MORE!

* The Korean War was fought between South Korea and North Korea from June 25, 1950, to July 27, 1953.

* The United States, Great Britain, and the United Nations all supported South Korea. The Soviet Union and the People's Republic of China both supported North Korea.

* Over 5 million soldiers and civilians lost their lives during the war.

Elsa

George and Joy Adamson
Took in three orphaned cubs,
Lions they had discovered
Near some African shrubs.
The smallest, named Elsa,
Was Joy's favorite of the three.
They loved to go for walks
And lounge under the trees.
When her sisters went to live
In a European zoo,
Elsa stayed in Kenya—
Joy just couldn't say adieu.
But one day after Elsa
Caused an elephant stampede,
Joy knew the next step
Was for Elsa to be freed.
For three whole months they worked
Teaching Elsa to survive
So that on the wild plains
She knew how to stay alive.
They taught her how to hunt,
And how to fight her foes,
And engage with other lions,
Till it was time to let her go.
They said good-bye and left her
With a lion pride.
And one day Elsa visited,
With three cubs by her side.
Joy went on to write
A book called *Born Free*
About her life with Elsa
That became a famed movie.

HISTORICAL STATS

FULL NAME: Elsa

BORN: January 1956 (Kenya, Africa)

DIED: January 24, 1961 (Kenya, Africa)

OCCUPATION: Wild animal turned pet turned wild animal

CLAIM TO FAME: Had her story told in a best-selling book and popular movie, both titled *Born Free*

DID YOU KNOW?

* After Elsa was released back into the wild, she gave birth to three cubs. She brought the cubs with her one day to show them to the Adamsons. They named her cubs Gopa, Jespah, and Little Elsa.

* In 1961, Elsa contracted a tick-borne blood disease called babesiosis. She died soon after. Her grave is located in Meru National Park.

* Joy Adamson wrote two more books about Elsa and her lion cubs entitled *Living Free* and *Forever Free*.

* Lions live in social groups called prides. A pride usually consists of two males, five females, and their offspring.

TELL ME MORE!

* The capital of Kenya is Nairobi. Nairobi is also the largest city in the country.

* Kenya is named after the highest mountain in the country, Mount Kenya. At 17,057 feet, it is also the second highest mountain in Africa (behind Kilimanjaro).

* When people visit Kenya, they usually go on a safari to see wild animals in national parks. The word *safari* is a Swahili word that means *journey*.

* The setting for the Disney film *The Lion King* is modeled after Hell's Gate National Park in Kenya.

Congo

Congo was a chimp
Living at the London Zoo.
But there was more to life
Than sitting there on view.
For Congo had a gift:
He loved to draw and paint.
His style was abstract,
Surrealist, yet quaint.
By the age of four
With four hundred works complete,
Congo had achieved
Quite amazing feats.
Around the world his paintings
Were displayed for all to see.
Even Picasso was a fan;
So was Salvador Dalí!

DID YOU KNOW?

* Congo began to draw at the age of two, when zoologist Desmond Morris gave him a pencil.

* From an early age, Congo showed an ability for drawing symmetrically. When Morris drew a shape on one side of a piece of paper, Congo would draw the same shape on the other side.

* In 2005, several of Congo's paintings were held at auction alongside works by Andy Warhol and Renoir. They sold for more than expected, while Warhol's and Renoir's paintings did not sell at all.

* If stopped before he deemed a painting finished, Congo would throw a screaming fit. Likewise, if coaxed to continue working on a "finished" painting, he would refuse.

* Humans and chimpanzees share 95 to 98 percent of the same DNA, making chimpanzees one of our closest living relatives.

* Chimpanzees are classified as an endangered species. Today there are only about two hundred thousand chimps living in the wild.

HISTORICAL STATS

FULL NAME: Congo

BORN: 1954 (unknown)

DIED: 1964 (London, England)

OCCUPATION: Abstract artist

CLAIM TO FAME: One of the greatest animal artists of all time

TELL ME MORE!

* Abstract art is a mixture of lines, shapes, and colors. Although there is no subject matter, it is still trying to convey some sort of emotion.

* The Abstract Expressionism movement began in the 1940s in New York City.

* Famous abstract artists include Mark Rothko, Jackson Pollock, and Wassily Kandinsky.

Belka and Strelka

Belka and Strelka
May have been strays,
But they were destined
For glory and praise.
Along with a rabbit,
Some mice and some rats,
Various flies,
Some fungi, and plants,
They were both sent
In a module to space
By the Soviet Union
To win the space race!

HISTORICAL STATS

FULL NAME: Belka and Strelka

BORN: Unknown

DIED: Unknown

OCCUPATION: Astronauts

CLAIM TO FAME: The first dogs to go into orbit and return safely to Earth

DID YOU KNOW?

* Belka and Strelka spent a day aboard Korabl-Sputnik-2 on August 19, 1960.

* The flight was broadcast on television. While Strelka often seemed stressed and on guard, Belka usually appeared happy.

* Stray dogs were selected for the mission because scientists felt they could handle the stresses of space flight better than other dogs.

* Only female dogs were used because of their milder temperaments, and because the space suits were designed so that only female dogs could go to the bathroom in them.

* Before the flight, each dog trained hard for the trip. They wore space suits, stood for long periods of time, and spent time inside simulators that acted like rockets during takeoff.

* The dogs quickly became celebrities, receiving fame and glory worldwide. They made appearances in schools and orphanages, entertaining kids and adults wherever they went.

TELL ME MORE!

* During the 1950s and 1960s, the USSR used dogs for suborbital and orbital space flights to see if humans could one day go into space.

* Both the USSR and the United States were trying to advance space technology at the same time. This competition is often referred to as the space race.

* Later in her life, Strelka gave birth to a litter of puppies. One of them, Pushinka, was given to President John F. Kennedy's daughter, Caroline.

Jane Goodall

Deep in the jungles of Tanzania,
A family of chimps lived in the trees.
Watching their humanlike interactions
Was Jane Goodall's main expertise.
They used tools, she observed,
To catch bugs to eat,
And she was surprised
To see them eat meat.
Socially speaking,
Chimps are like man:
They kiss and they hug
And even hold hands.
Yes, our chimpanzee brothers
Have similar ways.
Perhaps it's because
We share DNA.

DID YOU KNOW?

* Jane began studying families of chimpanzees in the Gombe Stream National Park in Tanzania in 1960. Her study lasted forty-five years.

* Her studies suggest that chimpanzees share many of the same emotions, intelligence, and social interactions as humans.

* Jane Goodall observed chimpanzees using more tools than any other animal. Some of these included long blades of grass to fish for termites and stones to break open nuts.

* She also discovered that chimpanzees are omnivores and eat meat as well as plants. Prior to her studying them, it was believed that they only ate plants.

* Chimpanzees live in communities that consist of up to sixty members.

HISTORICAL STATS

FULL NAME: Dame Jane Morris Goodall

BORN: April 3, 1934 (London, England)

OCCUPATIONS: Primatologist, anthropologist, ethologist, UN Messenger of Peace

CLAIM TO FAME: The world's foremost expert on chimpanzees

TELL ME MORE!

* When she was a little girl, Jane's father gave her a chimpanzee toy that began her love for animals. She still has the toy to this day.

* For a period of two years, she lived with the chimpanzees in their community.

* In 1977, she formed the Jane Goodall Institute to protect chimpanzees and their habitats.

Mr. Magoo

In nineteen sixty-three
In the city of Duluth,
A mongoose named Magoo
Faced an awful truth.
Turns out the animal
Is illegal in the states.
So an executioner came
To seal the creature's fate.
But people mobilized
To save poor Mr. Magoo.
They petitioned so that he
Could stay safely at the zoo.
The pleas reached the White House;
They were plentiful and rife.
And President JFK
Signed a pardon for his life.

DID YOU KNOW?

* The Duluth Zoo acquired Mr. Magoo when a foreign ship docked on the banks of the great lakes and the sailor donated his pet mongoose to them.

* Mongooses are illegal to keep in the United States because they breed too fast and have no known enemies. Customs officials ordered that Mr. Magoo be put down.

* The city of Duluth mobilized to save Mr. Magoo from the federal executioner. Petitions were signed, the mayor sought a court order for a stay of execution, and citizens wired their congressmen.

* On April 19, 1963, the Department of the Interior in Washington, DC, granted asylum to Mr. Magoo. President Kennedy supposedly said, "Let the story of the saving of Magoo stand as a classic example of government by the people."

* Mongooses mostly live in southern Asia, Africa, and southern Europe. They can also be found in some Caribbean and Hawaiian islands and Puerto Rico.

HISTORICAL STATS

FULL NAME: Mr. Magoo

BORN: Unknown

DIED: 1968 (Duluth, Minnesota)

OCCUPATION: Zoo animal

CLAIM TO FAME: Had his life spared by President Kennedy after being sentenced to death by the US Fish and Wildlife Service

TELL ME MORE!

* Today it is still illegal to import mongooses into the United States (with the exception of Hawaii).

* The US Fish and Wildlife Service is a federal agency within the US Department of the Interior. They are dedicated to the management of fish, wildlife, and natural habitats.

* The US Fish and Wildlife Service enforces federal wildlife laws, protects endangered species, and conserves habitats such as the wetlands.

Shamu

In the sixties in San Diego,
An orca named Shamu
Became the main attraction
At SeaWorld's marine zoo.
She'd jump and splash the crowds
And even give high fives.
People from all over
Came to watch her dive.
The show got high acclaim;
Shamu quickly rose to fame.
And today it's just the same:
She's still a household name!

DID YOU KNOW?

* The original Shamu was the first orca to survive more than thirteen months in captivity.
* After Shamu's death in 1971, the name Shamu continued to be used for different killer whales in different SeaWorld parks.
* Killer whales, or orcas, are actually the largest members of the dolphin family.
* Killer whales use echolocation to communicate and hunt. They make sounds that travel underwater, and when the sounds encounter an object, they bounce back, letting the killer whale know the object's location, size, and shape.
* Killer whales hunt in groups called pods and circle their prey before attacking. They prey on seals, sea lions, fish, birds, turtles, octopuses, squid, and other dolphins and whales.

HISTORICAL STATS

FULL NAME: Shamu

BORN: Unknown

DIED: August 1971 (San Diego, California)

OCCUPATION: Entertainer

CLAIM TO FAME: Star of the killer whale show at SeaWorld San Diego in the 1960s

TELL ME MORE!

* The first SeaWorld opened in San Diego on March 21, 1964. With only a few dolphins, sea lions, and six attractions, the park became a quick success. More than four hundred thousand people visited the park in the first twelve months.
* SeaWorld no longer captures killer whales from the wild. They obtain them through breeding, loans, and purchases from other marine parks.
* Some people believe keeping killer whales in captivity is wrong. Tank size, chemically altered water, and abnormal social groupings may make the animals stressed.

Secretariat

At the Kentucky Derby
In nineteen seventy-three,
Secretariat ran last
But was quickly gaining speed.
He passed Angle Light
And Sham at the stretch.
He came in first place!
The Preakness was next.
Again, he ran last,
Then moved to first place.
Past Sham, once again,
And Old Native he raced.
After coming in first,
More bets were placed
At the famed Belmont Stakes,
The next and final race.
He passed Private Smiles,
And Sham he wore down,
Then went on to win
The whole Triple Crown!

DID YOU KNOW?

* In 1973, Secretariat set records in all three races that still stand today.

* Ron Turcotte was the jockey who raced Secretariat to win all three races.

* Secretariat appeared on the covers of *Sports Illustrated*, *Time*, and *Newsweek* magazines the week before his Belmont Stakes race.

* Toward the end of his life, Secretariat suffered from laminitis, a hoof disease without a cure.

* Bronze statues of Secretariat can be found in Belmont Park, New York, at the Hall of Fame in Saratoga, New York, and at the Kentucky Horse Park, Kentucky.

* All racehorses share the same birthdays, regardless of when they were actually born. This helps keep track of their bloodlines. Northern hemisphere racehorses celebrate their birthdays on January 1, while the Southern hemisphere horses celebrate August 1.

HISTORICAL STATS

FULL NAME: Secretariat

BORN: March 30, 1970 (The Meadow in Doswell, Virginia)

DIED: October 4, 1989 (Claiborne Farms in Paris, Kentucky)

OCCUPATION: Racehorse

CLAIM TO FAME: The fastest Triple Crown champion to date

TELL ME MORE!

* The Triple Crown of Thoroughbred Racing is a series of three races: the Kentucky Derby, the Preakness Stakes, and the Belmont Stakes. A Triple Crown winner is a horse that wins all three races in a single year.

* At a mile and a half, the Belmont Stakes is the longest of the three races.

* Only eleven horses have ever won the Triple Crown, and none since 1978.

Koko

Koko, a gorilla,
Learned how to speak through signs.
She can talk with others,
Answer questions, even whine!
A woman, Penny Patterson,
Taught this curious beast
How to understand
A thousand signs at least!
One day Penny gifted
Koko with a kitten.
The gorilla named it All Ball
And right away was smitten.
She cared for him as if
He were her own offspring.
But a car killed poor All Ball,
And Koko felt the sting.
"Bad, sad, bad," she signed,
And cried alone in grief.
But, as time went on,
Her heart found some relief.
Two more kittens came
To live with her one day.
They were gray like All Ball,
And her sadness slipped away.

HISTORICAL STATS

FULL NAME: Koko

BORN: July 4, 1971 (San Francisco, California)

OCCUPATION: Communicator

CLAIM TO FAME: Can understand more than a thousand signs based on American Sign Language

DID YOU KNOW?

* Koko was born at the San Francisco Zoo and has lived most of her life in Woodside, California.

* Koko has even invented new signs to communicate. Once she signed "finger bracelet" when referring to somebody's ring.

* After All Ball's death, Koko was able to choose two new kittens to be her companions. Like All Ball, they were gray Manx cats, and she named them Lipstick and Smokey.

* There are three different types of gorillas, all named after areas in Africa: Mountain, Western Lowland, and Eastern Lowland. Koko is a Western Lowland gorilla.

TELL ME MORE!

* Different sign languages are used in different countries and regions.

* American Sign Language (ASL) contains all the fundamental features of language. It has rules for pronunciation, word order, and grammar.

* American Sign Language isn't a direct translation of English into hand gestures. It is its own language that uses the hands, arms, face, and head to convey meaning and emotion.

Dolly

At the U of Edinburgh
In Scotland, UK,
Dolly was born
The scientific way.
From another sheep
DNA was taken,
Put into a test tube
With an egg, then shaken.
Dolly was born soon after
And became well known
As the very first mammal
Ever to be cloned!

HISTORICAL STATS

FULL NAME: Dolly

BORN: July 5, 1996 (The Roslin Institute in Midlothian, Scotland)

DIED: February 14, 2003 (The Roslin Institute in Midlothian, Scotland)

OCCUPATION: Test subject

CLAIM TO FAME: First mammal to be cloned from an adult somatic cell

DID YOU KNOW?

* Dolly was the first mammal ever to be cloned from an adult somatic cell. Somatic cells make up a mammal's skin, bones, blood, tissue, and internal organs.

* Dolly had three mothers. One provided the egg, the second the DNA, and the third carried her to term.

* Dolly was named after the performance artist Dolly Parton.

* Dolly quickly became a household name after her birth was announced to the world. Media came from all over to have a look at the sheep.

* Sheep are pregnant for five months.

* The states that have the highest number of sheep are California, Texas, and Wyoming.

* Sheep are intelligent creatures. They can recognize up to fifty other sheep faces and remember them for two years. They can also recognize human faces.

* While in office, President Woodrow Wilson kept a flock of sheep at the White House.

TELL ME MORE!

* Since Dolly was successfully cloned, many other mammals, including pigs, deer, horses, and bulls, have also been cloned.

* Scientists are using cloning to preserve extinct and endangered species.

* The first dog to be cloned was born in South Korea in 2005 and was named Snuppy.

* Cloned animals do not always look identical to the animals whose DNA they share.

Paul the Octopus

Paul the Octopus
Could predict the winner
Of World Cup matches
Just by eating dinner.
Two boxes bearing flags
Were placed for the predictor
Within his Sea Life tank
For him to pick a victor.
The boxes each held food,
And whichever he first snatched
That country would go on
to win the next big match.
In the 2010 World Cup
Each team that he chose
Went on to win their games!
But how? Nobody knows.
He predicted many wins
For his home team, Germany,
But for the final game
He called a Spanish victory.
Spain was, in fact, triumphant;
They won against the Dutch.
And Paul went down in history
For his psychic touch.

DID YOU KNOW?

* After correctly predicting the 2010 World Cup, Paul received worldwide fame. International media covered Paul's predictions, and the video of him selecting Spain in the finals attracted hundreds of thousands of hits on YouTube.

* After Spain won the World Cup, angry fans of the losing team called for Paul to be cooked and eaten. In response, the Spanish prime minister offered Paul protection and safe haven in Spain. Despite the death threats, Paul remained in Germany.

* The foods that were placed in each of Paul's boxes were usually a mussel and a clam.

* An octopus has three hearts. Two of the hearts pump blood through their gills, and the third heart pumps blood throughout the rest of the body.

* Octopuses are deaf.

* The suckers on an octopus's arms can taste as well as feel.

* When under attack, octopuses can shed their arms to escape or distract predators. The arms will regenerate.

HISTORICAL STATS

FULL NAME: Paul the Octopus

BORN: 2008 (Sea Life Centre in Weymouth, England)

DIED: October 2010 (Sea Life Centre in Oberhausen, Germany)

OCCUPATION: Animal oracle

CLAIM TO FAME: Correctly predicted the outcomes of eight matches in the 2010 World Cup

TELL ME MORE!

* The FIFA World Cup soccer tournament is the world's most watched sporting event.

* Since the first tournament in 1930, the World Cup has been held every four years, except during World War II, when both the 1942 and 1946 tournaments were canceled.

* Currently, thirty-two countries compete in the World Cup.

* American Bert Patenaude scored the very first hat trick in the 1930 World Cup. A hat trick is when a player scores three goals in a single game.

Cairo

To hunt down a terrorist,
The US Navy found
A K9 dog named Cairo
To help them on the ground.
He sniffed for hidden bombs,
Kept civilians at bay,
And was ready to attack
If the enemy tried to stray.
Yes, Cairo was quite vital
In carrying out the mission.
Even President Obama
Gave him recognition.

HISTORICAL STATS

FULL NAME: Cairo

NICKNAME: The nation's most courageous dog

BORN: Undisclosed

OCCUPATION: Navy SEAL

CLAIM TO FAME: Used in Operation Neptune Spear to hunt down Osama bin Laden

DID YOU KNOW?

* Cairo is a Belgian Malinois, a breed similar to a German shepherd, but smaller and more compact.

* During the operation, Cairo's main role was to secure the building's perimeter. He made sure nobody from inside escaped and kept curious neighbors at bay.

* President Obama personally met Cairo in a private ceremony honoring the SEALs who participated in the operation.

* War dogs have been used by the Egyptians, Greeks, Persians, Sarmatians, Alans, Slavs, Britons, Romans, and others.

* Dogs have an 80 percent success rate in detecting explosive devices.

* A K9 dog is trained to assist law-enforcement personnel, such as the police or the military. *K9* is a homophone for the word *canine*.

TELL ME MORE!

* Operation Neptune Spear was carried out on May 1, 2011. A team of forty Navy SEALs hunted down and killed terrorist leader Osama bin Laden in Abbottabad, Pakistan.

* The US Navy SEALs were established by President John F. Kennedy. They are trained to operate in all the environments (SEa, Air, and Land) for which they are named.

* SEAL training is extremely difficult and has the reputation of being some of the toughest in the world.

Index

Also by Julia Moberg

It's been said that if you want a friend at the White House, get a dog. Or, we might add, perhaps a cat, bird, bear, or maybe an alligator! Throughout America's history, the presidential menagerie has included an array of creatures both big and small, ordinary and absurd.

This inside look at the White House's animal residents features a rollicking, rhyming verse for each commander-in-chief's pets, accompanied by cool facts, presidential stats, and laugh-out-loud cartoon art. John Quincy Adams kept an alligator in the bathtub, while Thomas Jefferson's pride and joy was his pair of bear cubs. Andrew Jackson had a potty-mouthed parrot, and Martin Van Buren got into a fight with Congress over his two baby tigers. First daughter Caroline Kennedy's pony Macaroni had free reign over the White House. But the pet-owning winner of all the presidents was Theodore Roosevelt, who had a hyena, lion, zebra, badger, snake, rats, a nippy dog that bit the French ambassador, and more!

- An IRA-CBC Children's Choice, 2013

- A Children's Book-of-the-Month Club Main Selection

- Moberg uses humor, trivia, and children's innate love of animals to bring to life the presidents and the history that surrounded their time in office. This is a book that readers can come back to over and over, enjoying different aspects of it each time and in a different order.
  —*School Library Journal*

- The mixture of straight nonfiction text, rhythmic verse, and vibrant graphics make this a versatile addition to any collection or classroom in need of a presidential trivia tome.
  —*Booklist*